REVISED AND UPDATED

HOW TO RAISE
Monarch Butterflies
A Step-by-Step Guide for Kids

BY CAROL PASTERNAK

FIREFLY BOOKS

This book is dedicated to Lawrence Fagan, who ignited our family's love of nature through the raising of monarch butterflies.

A FIREFLY BOOK

Published by Firefly Books Ltd. 2012

Copyright © 2012 Firefly Books Ltd.

Text copyright © 2012 Carol Pasternak

THIRD PRINTING, WITH UPDATES, 2017

Library and Archives Canada Cataloguing in Publication

Pasternak, Carol, 1954–
How to raise monarch butterflies / Carol Pasternak.

Includes bibliographical references and index.

ISBN-13: 978-1-77085-001-9 (bound)
ISBN-13: 978-1-77085-002-6 (pbk.)

1. Monarch butterfly—Juvenile literature. I. Title.

QL561.D3P37 2012   j595.78'9   C2011-906860-5

Publisher Cataloging-in-Publication Data (U.S.)

Pasternak, Carol.
How to raise monarch butterflies / Carol Pasternak.
[48] p. : col. photos., maps ; cm.

Includes bibliographical references and index.

Summary: Step-by-step instructions and color photographs explain the process of raising monarch butterflies.

ISBN-13: 978-1-77085-001-9
ISBN-13: 978-1-77085-002-6 (pbk.)

1. Monarch butterfly—Juvenile literature.
2. Monarch butterfly—Life cycles—Juvenile literature.
I. Title.

595.789 dc23   QL561.D3 2012

Published in the United States by
Firefly Books (U.S.) Inc.
P.O. Box 1338
Ellicott Station
Buffalo, New York 14205

Published in Canada by
Firefly Books Ltd.
50 Staples Avenue, Unit 1
Richmond Hill, Ontario
L4B 0A7

Cover and interior design:
LINDdesign

Printed in China

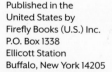

 Canada We acknowledge the financial support of the Government of Canada.

Contents

The Amazing Monarch

If you whisper a wish to a butterfly, then give it its freedom, the wish will be taken to the Great Spirit and granted.

—Native American Indian legend

The monarch butterfly is one of the world's most beloved insects. Majestic and beautiful, the monarch displays its distinctive orange and black markings as it glides by with outstretched wings. It doesn't bite, sting, carry disease, or eat our vegetables. It seems to exist just to delight us.

For some, monarchs are a sure sign of summer's arrival. For others, they are a symbol of good luck — released at weddings to send the happy couple on its way. Monarchs have also become an enduring symbol of transformation and hope. Imagine … a pudgy, wormlike insect crafts an exquisite chrysalis and is reborn less than two weeks later as the most beautiful queen of them all.

Even after its remarkable birth, the monarch continues to intrigue. The idea that this tiny wonder, weighing less than a dime, can take off and fly more than 2,000 miles (3,200 kms) to a place it's never been is simply fascinating. No wonder we are still searching for clues as to what guides this incredible journey.

You can be a part of the monarch miracle. Do you know you can actually hold a newborn monarch in the palm of your hand? Can you imagine watching its first flight? The best way to experience these thrills is to raise a monarch yourself.

You will love your new hobby. You'll know the joy of caring for a pet and watching it grow, and, when it's ready, you'll set it free to begin its life in the wild. This book will show you how. Before you get started, though, let's meet the monarch!

Monarchs can be found in North America, South America, Australia, New Zealand and some South Pacific islands.

5

Anatomy of a Monarch Butterfly

Monarchs are complicated insects. They start their lives looking one way, and change into something entirely different. And they do it in just under a month! The four stages of this transformation — called metamorphosis — are egg, caterpillar (larva), chrysalis (pupa), and butterfly (adult).

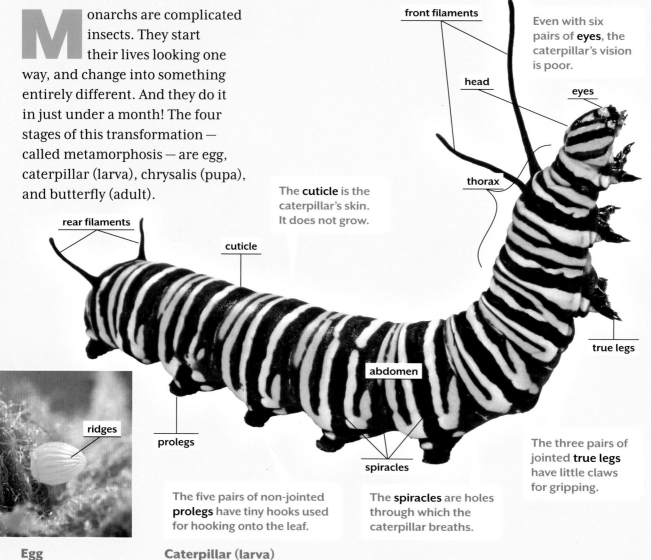

front filaments

Even with six pairs of **eyes**, the caterpillar's vision is poor.

head

eyes

thorax

The **cuticle** is the caterpillar's skin. It does not grow.

rear filaments

cuticle

true legs

abdomen

ridges

prolegs

spiracles

The three pairs of jointed **true legs** have little claws for gripping.

The five pairs of non-jointed **prolegs** have tiny hooks used for hooking onto the leaf.

The **spiracles** are holes through which the caterpillar breaths.

Egg

Caterpillar (larva)

silk pad

cremaster

abdominal segments

wings

head

Chrysalis (pupa)

The **proboscis** (pro-BOSS-is) is like a drinking straw. The monarch uses it to sip nectar.

A monarch's eye has thousands of individual lenses. A human eye has one.

fore wings

compound eye

antennae

thorax   head

leg

hind wings

proboscis

Monarch butterflies are deaf. Many associations for the hearing impaired use the butterfly as their symbol.

abdomen

Monarchs taste with their feet and smell with their antennae.

Butterfly (adult)

7

Raising Monarchs

This picture was taken at the garden center, where conditions are always perfect.

What You'll Need

Monarchs, like all moths and butterflies, belong to the order of insects called **Lepidoptera**. If you study or collect moths or butterflies, you are a **lepidopterist**.

Before you start your search for caterpillars or eggs, you'll want to make sure you're ready. Here's a list of things you'll need:

Plastic containers: You can buy plastic cages at a pet store, but you can also make your own. A big salad container with holes punched in the lid works well. So does an old aquarium, if you have one at home. The container should be lightweight for cleaning, and clear for viewing. It's a good idea to have more than one plastic container set aside, in case your first one gets too crowded. A smaller salad or take-out container is just right for your eggs.

Yogurt container or plastic bag: When you go out to gather your caterpillars or eggs, you'll want to make sure you have a safe way to get them home.

Scissors: You'll need these to cut leaves from the milkweed plant.

Paper towels or napkins: You'll need these to wrap the extra milkweed leaves you store in the fridge, and to line the "nursery" where you'll keep your monarch eggs.

Milkweed leaves: Whether you are starting with caterpillars or eggs, you will need a good, fresh supply of milkweed. Milkweed leaves are the only food monarch caterpillars will eat.

Damp cloth: If you accidentally get milkweed sap on your hands or face, wipe it off right away.

Magnifying glass: A magnifying glass is a great way to make sure you'll see every little thing there is to see.

Camera: If there's a camera in your house that you can use, bring it along. It doesn't need to be fancy —just a point-and-click model will do. Use it to capture your monarch's journey, right from the beginning.

Start with one or two small animal cages, available at most pet stores.

Yogurt container for collecting eggs and caterpillars.

Plastic containers with lids make good nurseries. Line them with a damp paper towel.

With a magnifying glass you can see every little thing.

Finding Caterpillars

Common milkweed blooms are usually pink. When you tear a leaf, you will see the milky sap running from it.

Now that you've gathered your materials, it's time to get started. The first thing you'll need to do is go on a hunt. Even if you live in a city, there are likely plenty of green spaces nearby.

Trek to the ravine, the trail, or the edge of the woods. Turn over a rock and see what scurries about in the bright light. Check out a rotting tree and discover tiny ant architects hard at work. Look up. Birds are soaring, darting, feeding their babies. Is there a rushing stream, colorful mushrooms, a small mammal? What's hanging out around the pond?

This is where your monarch adventure begins. You can start looking for the distinctive black, white, and yellow monarch caterpillars about a week after you spot the first monarchs in your area.

And there's only one place you need to look: on milkweed! Milkweed can be found in sunny open fields, by the park, on the shoulders of country roads, in the ravine, or in your own backyard, if you plant it. The most abundant milkweed is common milkweed. Its flowers are pink-purple. When you tear a leaf, you will see the milky sap running from it. That sap is bitter. That's why most animals won't eat milkweed. And since this is what caterpillars eat, they end up tasting bitter too, which is why most birds won't eat monarch caterpillars or butterflies.

When you find a caterpillar, cut off the leaf that it's on and place it in your yogurt container or plastic bag. Make sure to pick half a dozen extra leaves. When you get home, wrap the extra leaves in a damp paper towel, and then a plastic bag. Toss them in the fridge. They will stay fresh for several days.

WARNING Do not get sap in your eyes. It could sting for weeks. Clean your hands before touching your face.

When looking for caterpillars, watch for these telltale signs:

Chewed leaves

Even the smallest milkweed by the side of the road might host a big caterpillar!

Chewed buds

Greenish poops — called frass — on the leaves

Remember to check the underside of the leaf, where caterpillars often hide.

Young caterpillars love the new shoots at the top of the plant.

Taking Care of Your Caterpillars

Don't throw away your caterpillars! When cleaning your container, check each leaf carefully. Otherwise, you might be surprised the next time you open your recycling bin.

Once you have your caterpillars home, transfer them into a plastic container. Keep the container in the house, where you will see it often. Choose a brightly lit table away from direct sunlight. You should clean the container at least once a day. Just remove the leaves with the caterpillars on them and place them someplace safe. Dump the frass and the old leaves into the compost bin. Put in some fresh leaves, and then the leaves with the caterpillars. And remember to put the lid back on your container and click it shut. Otherwise, the caterpillars can escape.

Caterpillars must *always* have food, so you'll need to collect milkweed every few days. Remember to feed your caterpillars before you go to bed. While you're sleeping, they're eating.

Your monarch will emerge the morning after its chrysalis becomes clear. Start a new container for caterpillars. Soon after birth, the monarch will release a red fluid, called meconium. Your caterpillars do not want this landing on their heads! From time to time, and after your last batch, ask your parents to wipe out all your containers with a weak bleach solution. This will help prevent the spread of diseases.

If you have several caterpillars, you may find that your cage gets crowded as they grow. Add new cages, if you need to, and make sure you keep the tiny caterpillars separate from the big ones, or they might get eaten by mistake!

Taking care of your caterpillars is a big responsibility. You'll need to attend to them every day, just as you would to your puppy, goldfish, or hamster.

In less than two weeks, a monarch grows to 3,000 times its birth weight.

The Great Egg Hunt

If you just can't wait to start your adventure, you can start looking for monarch eggs as soon as the adults return to your area from their overwintering grounds. This would be March in Texas and June in Canada.

You'll have to look carefully, though! A monarch egg is smaller than a sesame seed. It's creamy white and the shape of a football. Monarchs lay their eggs only on milkweed, usually on the underside of the leaf. If you see a monarch laying an egg, go straight to the plant and carefully cut off the leaf with the egg on it.

Once you've gathered a few eggs, take them home to the nursery. Line your plastic container with a damp paper towel, then lay out your leaves, egg side up. Seal the container to keep the moisture in and help prevent the leaves from drying out.

Check the nursery every day for mold, and replace the lining when necessary. Always make sure your newborns have a fresh leaf to eat. If the leaf they are on is drying out or turning yellow, carefully cut around the newly emerged caterpillar (or egg) and place the piece on a new leaf.

Be patient, and enjoy the milkweed patch. You may have to turn over a hundred leaves or more to find an egg.

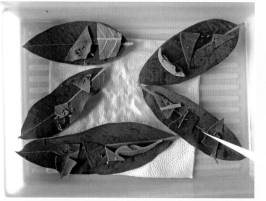

If you punch holes in the lid, the little ones might escape. They will get all the air they need when you open the container to remove excess moisture and check for mold.

Monarch eggs are most often found on the underside of a big leaf. However, you'll also need to look:

On the buds!

On the top of the big leaves.

All over the tiniest, previously mowed milkweed.

On the new leaves near the top of the plant.

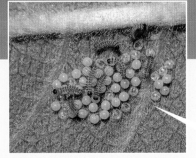

You might even find mystery eggs that another insect has laid on milkweed!

17

The Monarch Life Cycle

Here We Grow

Butterflies make **chrysalids**; moths make **cocoons**.

The baby caterpillar is about to emerge.

The first thing it does is eat its shell.

Now that your monarch eggs or caterpillars are safe in their containers, you can watch them grow and change. A monarch egg takes four or five days to hatch. Watch the egg carefully, using your magnifying glass. When the top of the egg is black, the baby caterpillar is about to emerge. Once the pale green caterpillar with the black head comes out, the first thing it does is eat its protein-rich shell.

When the caterpillar is born, it is barely the size of the writing on a dime. By day two, the caterpillar has doubled in size, although it's still only a fraction of the size of a sunflower seed. By day four, the caterpillar has doubled its size again. In another week it is in its final stage (or instar), ready to make a chrysalis. If you grew at the same rate as a caterpillar, in two weeks you'd be the size of a school bus!

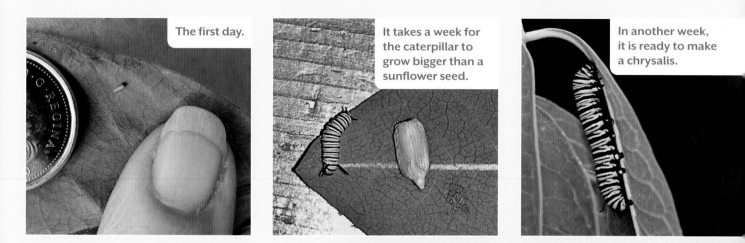

The first day.

It takes a week for the caterpillar to grow bigger than a sunflower seed.

In another week, it is ready to make a chrysalis.

All of this growing is hard work — especially if your skin doesn't grow along with you. Caterpillars burst out of their skin, or molt, four times before their final molt, when they pupate, or form a chrysalis. If your caterpillar doesn't seem to be moving much, don't worry; it's probably preparing to molt. Once it's ready — sometimes after a full day of inactivity — it spins a silk mat on a leaf or on the side or top of its container. Then it puffs itself up, crawls out of its old skin, and turns around and eats it!

It's best not to disturb your caterpillar during molting. It could die.

The Chrysalis

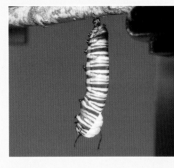

To rehang a fallen chrysalis use dental floss or a drop of glue.

When your caterpillar is 10 to 14 days old, it will stop eating and crawl to the top of the container in order to pupate. In the wild, the caterpillar will almost always leave its host milkweed at this stage, preferring a sturdy place that is sheltered from the wind and rain. First, the caterpillar will spin a silk button. Then it will turn around and attach itself to that button. Finally, the caterpillar will hang, head down, in a "J" shape. It will stay like this for about 14 hours.

If you watch the caterpillar carefully, you'll be able to tell when it's getting ready for its final molt. It will straighten slightly and its filaments will become twisted. Stay near to witness the spectacular transformation. The caterpillar will appear to unzip its skin and the pale green pupa will be exposed. Once the first crack in the caterpillar's skin appears, it takes less than two minutes for the pupa to appear. Over the next few minutes, the monarch pupa will continue to change by whirling and twirling in its "pupa dance." When the process is complete, the pupa will be a beautiful jade color with gold trim.

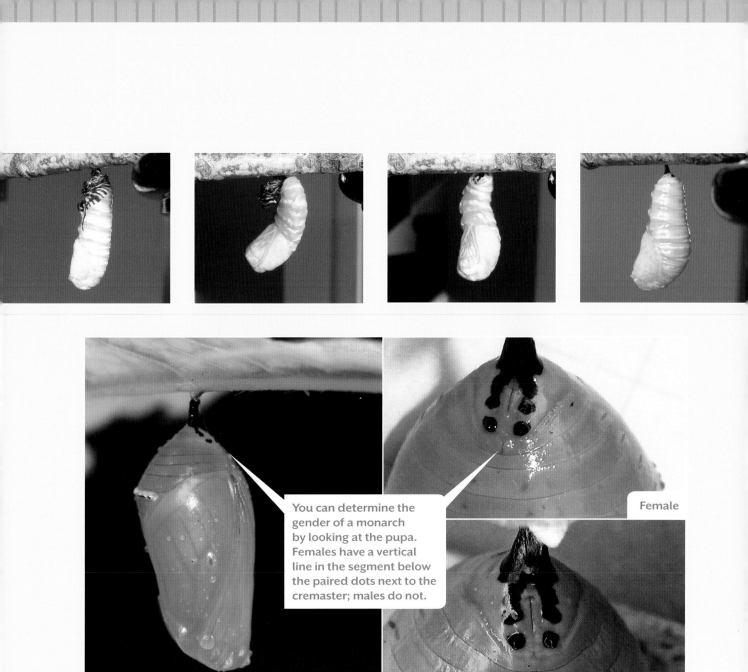

You can determine the gender of a monarch by looking at the pupa. Females have a vertical line in the segment below the paired dots next to the cremaster; males do not.

Female

Male

The Monarch Emerges

About an hour and a half after the monarch is born, it is strong enough to be handled, but not strong enough to fly. Put your finger gently under its front legs and it will crawl onto you. Have your camera ready.

A monarch will remain in the chrysalis state for one to two weeks. You can tell when something is about to happen by keeping a close eye on your chrysalis. About 24 hours before the monarch is ready to emerge, the bright green chrysalis will begin to darken and become transparent. You'll be able to see the monarch's beautiful orange and black wings inside. Monarchs usually emerge—or eclose—first thing in the morning, so if it looks like your chrysalis is changing, you may want to wake up early!

Once the first crack in the chrysalis appears, it takes only a minute for the monarch to pop out and hang from the chrysalis skin. The first thing the new butterfly does is stick out its long proboscis. Its wings will be crumpled, and the monarch will need to pump them full of fluids from its body, and then dry them. During this stage, it's important that the monarch is able to hang its wings freely, with nothing touching them. Otherwise, they may not form properly.

In less than half an hour, the butterfly will be fully expanded, although it will take several hours for it to prepare for its first flight. If it starts to flutter its wings, it's getting ready to take off!

It's a girl! The veins in her wings are darker than the male's.

It's a boy! He has a black spot on each of his hind wings.

Even with its wings closed, you can still tell that this is a male by the faint black smudge still visible on the vein of its hind wing.

Out in the World

Apartments and public gardens often have a good variety of well maintained flowers. Where will *you* take your monarchs two hours after they are born?

Releasing Your Butterfly

Share the fun! You will be the star of the show when you let your friends, neighbors, family members, and classmates hold and release one of your monarchs. It is an experience they will never forget. They will have questions, and you will feel so proud to be the expert.

When transfering your monarch from one place to another, make sure you let it crawl on or off your finger. Don't touch the wings while they are still drying.

Finally, it's in your hands! In just under a month, your insect has gone from egg to larva to pupa to adult. Now that it's a full-grown butterfly, it's time to set it free. It's safe to release your monarch three hours after it emerges.

A monarch often does not eat until the day after it's born, so if the weather is rainy or stormy, you can keep it overnight. If conditions still are not right, you will need to feed it before noon, and again later in the day. Mix one part honey with 10 parts water, or simply use Gatorade, the kind with sugar. You'll need to gently unfurl the proboscis with a toothpick or straightened paper clip the first time you feed it. After that, it will know what to do! Start with the toothpick under the monarch's chin, and gently press up and away from it. You can do it! Make sure the tip of the proboscis touches the liquid.

Once the monarch understands that it doesn't need a flower to feed, you can offer it scored fruit, like watermelon or orange slices, or a gatorade soaked cotton ball. Leave the meal in the flight cage and it will feed itself when it is hungry. Change daily.

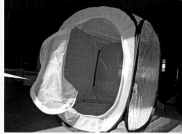

You can buy a flight cage like this, or simply use a mesh laundry basket.

If the sun is behind your monarch, you'll discover that its wings are translucent. That means the light can pass through them.

Two hours after its birth is a great time to photograph your butterfly. Keep your eyes open for photo ops. The backyard, the park at the corner, a nearby garden — almost anyplace will work. A simple point-and-click camera will do the trick. You can take most photos on the "automatic" setting, where the camera does the work for you. Take lots and lots of pictures. Zoom in, zoom out, move to the left or right, step forward or back. If you want to try close-ups, switch to the "macro" setting. It's fun to experiment.

Predators and Perils

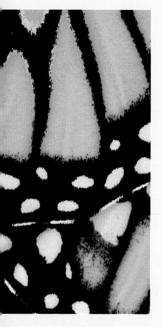

The monarch's distinctive orange and black coloring serves as a signal to potential predators, warning them of the butterfly's unpleasant taste.

When you bring home an egg or a caterpillar, you might actually be rescuing it. Only one in a hundred eggs in the wild survives to be an adult. Many are eaten by predators like spiders, ants and earwigs. Caterpillars are enjoyed by lady bugs, wasps, assassin bugs, spiders and other insects. Luckily for them, the unpleasant tasting milkweed sap they eat protects them from being eaten by birds, which choose other caterpillars to feed their babies.

Some of the caterpillars you find in the milkweed patch will be invaded by parasites. Tachinid flies have the nasty habit of laying *their* eggs on caterpillars, and tiny wasps lay their eggs right inside monarch eggs or pupae. Another threat is *Ophryocystis elektroscirrha*—or OE, for short. The culprit is a single-celled organism, or protozoa, so small you can't see it. Monarchs that are infected with

OE are weak and may have difficulty emerging from the chrysalis. Some die before they emerge.

As adult butterflies, monarchs continue to provide meals for spiders and wasps, plus a whole new range of diners, including dragonflies, lizards, frogs, praying mantids and even cats!

When they get to their overwintering grounds, there are a few species of birds and mice that feast on them while they roost. Each bird or mouse can consume up to 40 monarchs per visit.

The monarch's bitter taste does not deter dragonflies.

Spiders can ensnare butterflies in their webs, or pounce on an unsuspecting caterpillar.

Tachinid fly larva

Wasps are predators to many insects, including monarch butterflies and caterpillars.

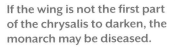

If the wing is not the first part of the chrysalis to darken, the monarch may be diseased.

Mating and Migration

Each year, millions of migrating monarchs arrive in Mexico around November 1, which has been celebrated in Mexican cultures for generations as "The Day of the Dead." Many Mexicans believe the returning butterflies carry the souls of their ancestors.

It may seem as if all the monarch's energy is taken up with survival, but in fact, the adult's main job is to reproduce— to mate and lay the eggs that will become the next generation.

Monarchs first mate when they are at least three days old. Females begin laying eggs right after their mating, and both sexes will mate several times during their lives. Over the course of her life, a female monarch can lay between 400 and 500 eggs.

In the early summer generations, adults live for only two to five weeks. But the final generation of monarchs is different. This group, which emerges in late summer and early fall, lives longer—for eight or nine months. Why? These butterflies have an important task. They must migrate to the overwintering grounds, either in central Mexico (for eastern monarchs) or in California (for western monarchs).

How do monarchs know when it's time to migrate? The days get shorter, the nights get cooler, and the milkweed gets old. When this happens, the monarchs don't mate. Instead, they tank up on goldenrod or other nectar in preparation for the long journey south.

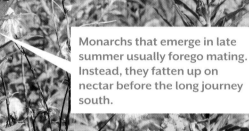

Monarchs that emerge in late summer usually forego mating. Instead, they fatten up on nectar before the long journey south.

Monarchs that emerge in early summer start to mate when they are three days old.

By the time milkweed pods explode in Canada, most of the monarchs are on their way south.

The Incredible Journey

How can a tiny insect fly 25 miles (40 km) in one day? It takes advantage of thermal updrafts and tailwind.

The monarchs' journey is incredible. The butterflies travel up to 2,500 miles (4,000 km) to a place they've never been. They average 25 miles (40 km) a day, facing all sorts of perils. Illnesses and infections can be fatal. They get hit by cars, and sprayed by insecticide. They have to deal with bad weather along the way, and at their destination. A harsh winter "down south" can be deadly.

Once they reach Mexico or California, the monarchs form large clusters, which in Mexico can number more than 50 million butterflies. They will roost there for four or five months, changing positions when necessary, and occasionally feeding or drinking when their reserves run low.

As spring approaches, the monarchs are instinctively driven to fly north to find fresh spring milkweed. They start to mate and lay eggs. Soon, this generation's lifespan will come to an end. It will take two generations to complete the return to the northern breeding habitats.

Many scientists have contributed to our knowledge of the monarch, including Dr. Fred Urquhart. In 1975, Urquhart—with the help of his wife Nora, thousands of volunteers, and decades of tagging research—mapped out the migration of the eastern monarchs. Before that, the monarchs' winter whereabouts were a mystery to Canadians and Americans.

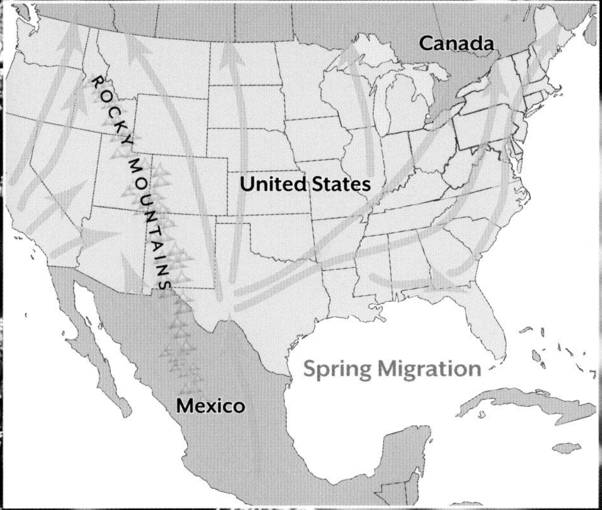

Fall Migration

Spring Migration

In Mexico, the monarchs roost on oyamel trees. The oyamel is a type of fir tree that is native to the mountains of central and southern Mexico. The monarchs that overwinter in California roost in many kinds of trees, including pines, palms, oaks and Eucalyptus.

Siena DiFrancesco,
Monarch enthusiast

Carter Steadman, Monarch
Advocate, West Virginia

Don Davis, Canada's foremost
monarch citizen scientist

Daniel Bravo, Monarch
Advocate, Florida

The Adventure Continues

Jim and Sheila Ellis,
Prolific taggers, Canada

Barbara Fagan,
Monarch enthusiast

Mynne Pasternak,
Monarch enthusiast

Audrey Kouyoumdjian,
Monarch enthusiast

Creating a Butterfly Garden

Monarchs and other butterflies love sunflowers, black-eyed Susans, goldenrod, blazing star, zinnias, wild bergamot and purple coneflower (Echinacea), pictured below.

Once you release your butterflies, you may want to learn how you can attract butterflies to your own garden next year. What's the best way to encourage guests to visit your home? Offer them food, of course. Set up your own wildlife buffet and you'll be rewarded with different kinds of butterflies, as well as a variety of interesting birds, bees and caterpillars.

Here's how:

Plant native flowering plants. Many butterflies and native flowering plants have co-evolved over time and depend on each other for survival and reproduction. Add some annuals like zinnias or Mexican sunflowers to provide nectar all season long. It's best to avoid butterfly bush if it is invasive in your area. It could crowd out the necessary native plants on which other insects lay their eggs. **The population of monarchs has plummeted. Be a part of the solution. Plant Milkweed!**

Include host plants. Butterflies lay their eggs on specific plants, called hosts. The resulting caterpillars then eat the leaves. Visit **gardenswithwings.com** and type in your zip code. You'll get an illustrated list of butterflies in your area and the plants you'll need to attract them.

Provide nectar all summer long. Monarchs need nectar all the time, so choose plants that bloom in early, mid and late summer.

Provide a place to rest. Butterflies need sun for orientation and to warm their wings for flight. Flat stones offer them a spot to rest and bask in the sun.

Avoid insecticides. These products kill insects, like caterpillars and butterflies.

Include water. Butterflies often congregate on wet sand and mud to partake in puddling—drinking water and extracting minerals from damp areas of the ground. Place coarse sand in a shallow pan and then insert the pan in the soil of your habitat. Keep the sand moist. Your monarchs will also enjoy a sip of water from the edge of the birdbath. Change the water every other day to avoid breeding mosquitoes.

Monarch puddling for minerals.

Eastern black swallowtail on dill.

American lady on pearly everlasting.

Eastern black swallowtail on black-eyed Susans.

Bee on ironweed.

Tiger swallowtail on chives.

The Milkweed Community

Monarchs lay their eggs *only* on milkweed.

Get as much of the rhizome (horizontal root) as you can.

We know that monarchs require milkweed, so you'll want to start your butterfly garden with at least two species. There are more than 100 species native to North America. To find the ones best suited to your area, see plantmilkweed.org

The milkweed most used by monarchs is Common Milkweed, and the best time to plant it is in the Fall. Gather seed pods when they are brown and splitting open. Separate the fluff from the seeds. Choose a place that gets a lot of sun, then rake them into the ground, or cover with just a quarter of an inch of soil.

If you're not ready to plant your seeds yet, let them dry for a few days, then store them in a glass jar in a cool dark place. Then, six weeks before you are ready to plant, mix them with sand and a spoon of water and put them in the fridge. This is called "cold moist stratification." In order to germinate, the seeds need to "think" they have been in the field for the winter.

Sometimes you can start milkweed without seeds. In the spring, you could dig up a small plant, making sure you dig deep. You don't want to cut the horizontal root, called the rhizome. New plants can also be started from some milkweeds, simply by putting a cutting in water and letting new roots grow.

Some people avoid common milkweed because it spreads more than they would like it to. In that case, plant it in a wild area near where you live, and choose other varieties for your garden, school, place of worship, community centre and workplaces. They can be beautiful, fragrant and long lasting, and when you choose native plants, they require so little attention once you have planted them. You could even grow some in a large planter on your balcony!

Milkweed bugs

Butterfly weed

Milkweed beetles

Swamp milkweed

Tussock moths

Ladybug and aphids

Saving the World for Butterflies

I wrote this book with the hope that you would experience the thrill of holding a magnificent monarch butterfly in your hands. Your new hobby will take you out of the house and into the wild, where you just might find yourself loving everything that grows, creeps, swims and flies.

As your love of nature grows, you'll likely find that you want to protect the environment—and maybe butterflies in particular. Did you know that just one generation ago, butterflies of all colors and sizes decorated the skies? Today, too many regions have seen a sharp decline in species and numbers. People need places to live and work, and that takes away from the habitat butterflies need to survive.

—Carol Pasternak,
The Monarch Crusader

How can we help?
Try these ideas:

- **Convert lawns into native plant gardens.** What's so great about grass? Convert part of your lawn to native plants. Encourage others in your neighborhood, such as schools, community centers and apartment and office buildings, to do the same. It will save time and money, and everyone will love the abundant wildlife.

- **Write letters to newspapers and politicians to explain the plight of the monarchs.** Encourage them to support laws to preserve wildlife habitats.

- **Teach.** Share your experience with your school, club, or public library. Write me for my free slide presentation and script. You can do it! monarchcrusader@gmail.com.

Certified Monarch Way Station

- **Support organizations that work to conserve butterflies.** Check out Monarch Watch (**monarchwatch.org**) and the Monarch Butterfly Fund (**monarchbutterflyfund.org**). Tag a monarch, become an expert, be an ambassador, make a donation or organize a fundraiser.

I'm counting on people just like you to help save the world for butterflies, for other animals and insects and for yourself.
Discover it. Love it. Protect it.

Want to Learn More?

Hopefully, this book has inspired you to want to learn more about the amazing monarch. If so, there are lots of places to look for additional information. A good place to start is my website, monarchcrusader.com. It will link you easily to all the best monarch sites and show you how to become a junior crusader for the monarch.

Don't be fooled! This monarch imposter is a viceroy.

Websites

monarchwatch.org
Information on everything you'll ever want to know about monarchs, including raising, tagging, migration and much more.

monarchteachernetwork.org
A full range of monarch-based curricula and activities.

fs.fed.us/wildflowers/ pollinators/monarchbutterfly
A comprehensive United States government website with materials for teachers, biology, conservation, activities and a full list of research papers, books, organizations and field guides.

learner.org/jnorth/monarch
Journey North is an outstanding website for teachers and students, with lesson plans, migration updates, FAQs, maps and more.

gardenswithwings.com/ what-is-a-butterfly-garden
If you live in the United States, just enter your zip code on this site. You'll get a list of butterflies in your region, and all the information you'll need to attract them.

monarchjointventure.org
Works with other groups to protect the monarch migration. Detailed information and print materials on a wide range of monarch topics.

butterflywebsite.com/ gardens This is a worldwide listing of butterfly gardens and conservatories.

monarchbutterflyfund.org
This organization focuses on protecting the oyamel forests in Mexico.

monarchparasites.org
Information on monarch parasites, and other reasons your caterpillars may be sick.

butterflybreeders.org
If you want to raise monarchs and cannot find them in the wild, you learn where to buy eggs, caterpillars and supplies here.

Book

Milkweed, Monarchs and More by Ba Rae and others. Have fun on every visit to the milkweed patch by discovering and learning about all the members of the milkweed community.

Facebook Group

The Beautiful Monarch This is the best place to get your everyday questions answered quickly, learn more, and share your journey.

Monarchs need to hang for several hours, first to pump their wings with fluid, then to let them dry.

Topics for Discussion

Here is a list of questions you might want to consider. Jot down your own answers or raise these questions in class. Use websites and books to find out more.

1. Why should we care about monarchs?

2. Would you like to see monarchs released at a wedding? Why or why not?

3. People in Mexico are cutting down oyamel trees. Why do you think that is, and what should be done?

4. What is the best thing you've ever seen in the woods, along the trail, in the countryside, in a meadow or the ravine?

5. Why is it important to have mostly native plants in your garden?

6. What kinds of things can you or your school do to raise awareness of monarch butterflies?

Glossary

chrysalis the stage in which the larva transforms into an adult.

cocoon a silk casing spun by many moth caterpillars.

cremaster the black stem on top of the chrysalis.

drought a prolonged period of abnormally low rainfall.

eclose to emerge as an adult from the chrysalis or as a larva from the egg.

frass the poo from the larva.

germinate to begin to grow and put out shoots.

habitat the natural home of an animal or plant.

instar the stage between molts.

invasive plants plants that have been introduced to an area from somewhere else. They spread and crowd out native plants.

irrigate to supply water so that plants will grow.

larva the stage between the egg and the pupa; for our purposes, the caterpillar.

migration when insects and animals travel over long distances.

molt when animals cast off their skins during their lifecyles.

native plants plants that occur naturally and have existed for many years in an area.

oviposit to lay an egg.

parasite an organism that lives in or on another organism and feeds off the host's body.

predators animals that eat other animals.

proboscis the monarch's long sucking tube. It looks like a tongue, but it is more like a drinking straw.

protozoa a single-celled microscopic organism.

pupa the stage in which the larva transforms into an adult, more commonly used for moths.

roost to settle down to rest or sleep.